TO BELONG

My Seed in the Ground Speaks Louder than Any Enemy's Voice

To Ms Follow with Love !

REMNANT CHILD

ISBN 978-1-0980-8431-8 (paperback)
ISBN 978-1-0980-8432-5 (digital)

Christian Faith Publishing, Inc.
832 Park Avenue
Meadville, PA 16335
www.christianfaithpublishing.com

Printed in the United States of America

First I must thank God for being my rock, my strength, my shield, and my hiding place! God supplied my every need according to his words.

Nothing missing in my life, nothing broken.

I have never known that I have something that I need to grow and give birth to until I have met with someone that is uncommon to other people!

A pastor, a teacher, an intercessor who prays on his knees that we could stand and a facilitator for God's people who acknowledges his anointing.

My spiritual father, Alph Lukau, and Mummy Celeste Lukau who stands with our father. I perceive that God has deposited something supernatural in him and cause the world to tremble at his existence on earth. God-man—that's what I called him.

One of his favorite quotes is "The anointing that you do not honor cannot sustain you." I can attest to this as one of his products who grabs it and runs with it!

My beloved children—Monique, Anashia, and Rochanda—are the fruits of God's reward. He has blessed me with a provocation of his Word to be made manifest in my life. My beloved granddaughter, Meilani, and the other grandchildren and great-grand coming as a generation of knowledge as God endowed for the future, I love you all!

My beloved husband, Brian, and our marriage that tested me beyond the depth of the flesh—to bring out the true anointing that was buried in me. The pureness of God's gift arises in me to dismantle the deception of the devil and his acolytes that tried to derailed me from my calling in God.

My amazing Aunt Sadie, Jasmine, and Kasita, my prayer partners when any spiritual fishiness arises to call on, as a tower of warfare weapons, we break down any Wall of Jericho with fasting and prayers. No stubborn devil can stand when we start as a group of warriors in Christ!

My beloved Mother Eunice, you did not have an easy life growing up, yet you keep pushing forward! May you reach the mark of the high calling of Christ in God!

My beloved sisters—Paulette, Sophia, Merline, Rosemare, Nicole, Rosalie, Lashana, Michelle, Christal—and those that are not mentioned, continue to stand on the Word of God! My brothers—Leo, who believes in me and there's no wrong that I can do in his eyes —Steve, Rohan, Floyd, Kingsley Jr., Marlon, Kirkroy, and Jay. Aunt Nelly, Una Lenora, Carlene, Jasmine, Imogene, Edith, Doreen, Zenna, and other aunts, you are so many to call by name; so I am just going to acknowledge that you are still here! To all my nieces and nephews and grandnieces and grandnephews not mentioned by name, not forgetting you all!

> If people don't occasionally walk
> away from you shaking their heads,
> you're doing something wrong.
> —John Gierach

Chapter 1

Judgment Begins in the House of God

"It is time for the church to arise again! Judgment must begin in the house of the Lord God Almighty."

Don't keep silent as God also calls us into a place of humility and loves us as we should love one another!

Do you know how many persons are dead and buried with secrets that are an asset to another person? I do! Let not the way a person think defy you! A lot of people would tell you today that they love you and all that you are going through. Put on a silver platter before them; give them the chance to examine it and let you know what they think of your situation. When they are examining it, they wait until you are dead to give the answer! I don't want to be one of those persons. The Bible tells me that there is no repentance in the grave. So whatsoever I am about to give to a person or invest in another, I will do the will of God now!

As we forsake the things in the kingdom of God, just remember the kingdom of God suffers violence and the violence taken by force. We as sons and daughters of God must examine ourselves as God calls us to be righteous people in his house to keep his statue and live upright before him.

And Samuel said to Saul, "You have done foolishly. You have not kept the commandment of the Lord your God, which He commanded you. For now the Lord would have established your kingdom over Israel forever. But now your kingdom shall not continue. The Lord has sought for

Himself a man after His own heart, and the Lord
has commanded him to be commander over His
people, because you have not kept what the Lord
commanded you." (1 Samuel 13:13–14)

It's time to look up redemption draweth nigh; it's time to cry
out Abba Father. It's time to pray. I realize we must be cautious when
interpreting current events of what's happening now and the natural
disasters around the world. A lot of people love to quote this scrip-
ture: "The rain falls on the just and on the unjust." Bad things often
happen to good people for no obvious reason. How can one know
whether a person is good or bad; only God knows because the heart
of men is desperately wicked. But God has not called us to speak
without a sound biblical basis for what we are seeing that is happening around us today. There are more than many reasons why most of
us Christians believe God's patience may be running out now faster
than before because of the desperation of people making things manifest presently around the world that has nothing to do with God.
The Bible said that all good things come from above!

The law of men is clear to the people that there are offices of
all types around the world opening, but there is a limit that is put to
restrain the work of God. Parliaments are open and so is the house of
representatives around the world. There are desires to everything you
can think of—desire to have a wedding, desire to party, and desire to
do all the things that have nothing to with God!

But as David said, "One thing that I desire is that I may dwell
in the house of the Lord forever, and to inquire in his temple and, to
behold the beauty of the Lord" (Psalm 27–4).

The heart is deceitful above all things, And
desperately wicked; Who can know it? I, the
Lord, search the heart, I test the mind, Even to
give every man according to his ways, According
to the fruit of his doings. (Jeremiah 17:9)

Every good gift and every perfect gift is from above, and cometh down from the Father of lights, with whom is no variableness, neither shadow of turning. (James 1:17)

And the rest of the men which were not killed by these plagues yet repented not of the works of their hands, that they should not worship devils, and idols of gold, and silver, and brass, and stone, and of wood: which neither can see, nor hear, nor walk: Neither repented they of their murders, nor of their sorceries, nor of their fornication, nor of their thefts. (Revelation 9:20)

And said, If thou wilt diligently hearken to the voice of the LORD thy God, and wilt do that which is right in his sight, and wilt give ear to his commandments, and keep all his statutes, I will put none of these diseases upon thee, which I have brought upon the Egyptians: for I [am] the LORD that healeth thee. (Exodus 15:26)

We were in South Africa in 2018 after a forty-day fasting, and the glory of God was everywhere. People have been healed from all sorts of diseases. And it took one set of devils to make one wicked comment, and it looked like the forty-day fasting was just in vain! People were shouting, crying, pleading with God for more of him; and the glory of God's glory was everywhere. I have never heard so many tongues spoken to God in my entire life. The demons were convulsing and screaming and coming out as the fire of God was consuming things, and some were even beside me, where I was standing with raised hands. Others were on their knees, and still others were prostrated on the floor. Some were rolling and just seeking God. Have you ever noticed that whenever God showed up in any place, it made a big difference? I have seen it multiple times! But I can tell you that when I got home to America, this only break bondages and chains that the devils were using upon God's people especially mine.

How time flies so fast! Oh my, it's that time already; we are in another year and another forty days of fasting again. All roads lead to International Visitor Program (IVP) Conference, for thousands of people had come in from all nations around the world to attend. We need more of God's people to continue to pray like the prophet Elijah, who called fire from heaven, and Joshua, who commanded the sun and the moon to be still. The people who know their God shall be strong and do exploits. God asked Job, "Have you commanded the morning since your days began, And caused the dawn to know its place, That it might take hold of the ends of the earth, And the wicked be shaken out of it?"

A commitment that perseveres over any and every obstacle until heaven is moved and nations are changed. At the end of the year, after crossing over into great grace from 2019 into a very special time in 2020, our spiritual Father had told us that the Lord has spoken to him about the great grace that is coming in 2020. I was thinking about the material aspect of life. I embark on my journey to South Africa at the end of February 2020 and en route from Amsterdam to South Africa to get there before the crowd coming from around the world. I arrived in South Africa and got to my hotel and checked in as the flight was an eventual one.

I could not wait to see what this fasting would bring out in me. It was very trying just thinking about the thousands of people coming from everywhere around the world that you can think of. I could imagine how it will impact me either way because the year before, I was there, and the overflow of people outside would not be good for me. So I was getting a little excited to go earlier than usual because we are closing our forty-day fasting and we are so blessed with all the spiritual gifts from God. I love to love Jesus! As we walk in the abundance of grace, that we know God in our everyday lives and search out the deep things of God whether here at home or around the world.

I have worked in the hospital for a number of years and rehabilitation where I work with people from all races and religion. There were times when you would sit with them and speak about all types of things, and they would enjoy the conversation until you touch how God is a merciful God to me, or to them. I realize that people would rather serve a different kind of God where there are no consequences in anything that they do. Whenever I am trying to have them to try to know the God of signs and wonders, they would tell me that God has never done anything for them. I would come back the next day, and there are different topics. And oh, it sounds wonderful, but just don't talk about this loving God that they cannot see in their condition lying in the hospital. This is the wages of sin talked about in the Bible.

I had one patient that was so mean when I met her in the hospital until she was transferred to the rehabilitation center. I came in for a twelve-hour shift, eight to eight. On the first night at the rehabilitation center, she checked in, and they gave her a room with a view. It was a split shift, so someone else would come in, in the day so that I could go home. Each night at work, she would complain so much for nothing because she does not want you to get too comfortable. Ward hours of the morning, she would check every hour to see if I was sleeping by calling out my name loudly. I would watch her and keep quiet because I didn't want her to wake up everyone else in the building. I would ask her if she was okay. She would say yes, and I would ask her if she would like anything. And she would refuse, or sometimes she would accept. This is going on for a while because she was going to be there for two months.

Now this was the second week, and she continued to behave the same way, kept calling out my name. One morning about 3:00 a.m., she kept calling me without stopping, and I did not answer her for about ten minutes.

When I did answer her, I said, "Yes?"

She said, "What are you doing?"

I said, "I am praying for you!"

After that morning, she has never tried to torment me again and left me alone!

I have proven God so many times it is uncountable! The only time I realize you can mention God to some of these people is when there's unbearable pain that the morphine can't help them with. As they think that this is it, the end, they start to call on God! Is God the last resort in your lives?

Can God truly bring back this generation to believe that he is the only true God? I dare not think the Lord God Almighty who bargains with Abraham for the souls of one hundred and comes down to ten people in the days of Sodom and Gomorrah. And God only got four souls, and one turned into a pillar of salt. My God who sits on the throne with all power in his hands would not leave his people pondering for a way out of this virus. From Passover, the Lord of the harvest showed up and brought us back to a place where we can process the fountain of life. We have seen how God works, and those of us that know him can speak how marvelous he is.

> For men shall be lovers of their own selves, covetous, boasters, proud, blasphemers, disobedient to parents, unthankful, unholy, without natural affection, trucebreakers, false accusers, incontinent, fierce, despisers of those that are good, Traitors, heady, highminded, lovers of pleasures more than lovers of God; Having a form of godliness, but denying the power thereof: from such turn away. For of this sort are they which creep into houses, and lead captive silly women laden with sins, led away with divers lusts, ever learning, and never able to come to the knowledge of the truth. Now as Jannes and Jambres withstood Moses, so do these also resist the truth: men of corrupt minds, reprobate concerning the faith. But they shall proceed no further: for their folly shall be manifest unto all men, as theirs also was. (2 Timothy 3)

> If my people, which are called by my name, shall humble themselves, and pray, and seek my face, and turn from their wicked ways; then will

I hear from heaven, and will forgive their sin,
and will heal their land. Now mine eyes shall be
open, and mine ears attent unto the prayer that
is made in this place. For now have I chosen and
sanctified this house, that my name may be there
for ever: and mine eyes and mine heart shall be
there perpetually. And as for thee, if thou wilt
walk before me, as David thy father walked, and
do according to all that I have commanded thee,
and shalt observe my statutes and my judgments.
(2 Chronicles 7:14)

I could remember the prime minister of Spain when this virus
started, without any hope or ways to help the people who are infected
with the virus. People had no clue of how this virus was spread, and
everyone was trying to figure out what's next. People were dying like
there is no tomorrow because no one could figure out the cause and
know what was going on. There was something of an invisible hand
snatching the people from the face of the earth.

"We have lost control. We have killed the epidemic physically
and mentally. Can't understand what more we can do. All solutions
are exhausted on ground. Our only hope remains up in the sky. God,
rescue your people." The Italian prime minister has said his country
has exhausted all options to fight against the coronavirus pandemic
and pleads to God to "rescue your people."

Then the Lord answered Job out of the
whirlwind, and said: "Who is this who darkens
counsel by words without knowledge? Now pre-
pare yourself like a man; I will question you, and
you shall answer Me. "Where were you when I
laid the foundations of the earth? Tell Me, if you
have understanding. Who determined its mea-
surements? Surely you know! Or who stretched
the line upon it? To what were its foundations
fastened? Or who laid its cornerstone, When the

morning stars sang together, and all the sons of God shouted for joy? "Or who shut in the sea with doors, When it burst forth and issued from the womb; When I made the clouds its garment, and thick darkness its swaddling band; When I fixed my limit for it, and set bars and doors; That thou shouldest take it to the bound thereof, and that thou shouldest know the paths to the house thereof? Knowest thou it, because thou wast then born? Or because the number of thy days is great? Hast thou entered into the treasures of the snow? Or hast thou seen the treasures of the hail, which I have reserved against the time of trouble, against the day of battle and war? (Job 38:1–10, 22)

If you are walking and you do not encounter the devil, be careful; you may be walking with him and don't know!

But Moses and Aaron fell facedown and said, "O God, the God of the spirits of all flesh, when one man sins, will You vent Your wrath on the whole congregation?" (Numbers 16:22)

Then the word of the Lord came to Jeremiah, saying, "Behold, I am the Lord, the God of all flesh. Is there anything too hard for Me? (Jeremiah 32:26)

Revelation of God to Me

Saints in Christ, during this lockdown of the COVID-19 virus, God has been opening his people's spiritual eyes to see the lies and the deception that are imposed upon his people. I am in New York; of course I am in the heart of the city that never sleeps! Have you ever wondered about the things that suddenly erupt in our daily lives and cripple the everyday things that we find pleasure in daily? While I am at home watching endless TV shows, I had an epiphany of how the world changes, and it is formed to engulf the very existences of the everyday lives of innocent people who cannot recognize that the plan that God has for them has been violated.

> Know ye not that the unrighteous shall not inherit the kingdom of God? Be not deceived: neither fornicators, nor idolaters, nor adulterers, nor effeminate, nor abusers of themselves with mankind, Nor thieves, nor covetous, nor drunkards, nor revilers, nor extortioners, shall inherit the kingdom of God. And such were some of you: but ye are washed, but ye are sanctified, but ye are justified in the name of the Lord Jesus, and by the Spirit of our God. (1 Corinthians 6:9–11)

> For thus saith the LORD, that after seventy years be accomplished at Babylon I will visit you, and perform my good word toward you, in causing you to return to this place. For I know the thoughts that I think toward you, saith the LORD, thoughts of peace, and not of evil, to give you an expected end. Then shall ye call upon me, and ye shall go and pray unto me, and I will hearken unto you. And ye shall seek me, and find me, when ye shall search for me with all your heart. And I will be found of you, saith the LORD: and I will turn away your captivity, and I will gather you from all the nations, and from all the places whither I have driven you, saith the LORD; and I will bring you again into the place whence I caused you to be carried away captive. (Jeremiah 29:10–14)

Dare any of you, having a matter against another, go to law before the unjust, and not before the saints? Do ye not know that the saints shall judge the world? And if the world shall be judged by you, are ye unworthy to judge the smallest matters? Know ye not that we shall judge angels? How much more things that pertain to this life? If then ye have judgments of things pertaining to this life, set them to judge who are least esteemed in the church. I speak to your shame. Is it so, that there is not a wise man among you? No, not one that shall be able to judge between his brethren? But brother goeth to law with brother, and that before the unbelievers. Now therefore there is utterly a fault among you, because ye go to law one with another. Why do ye not rather take wrong? Why do ye not rather suffer yourselves to be defrauded? Nay, ye do wrong, and defraud, and that your brethren. And such were some of you: but ye are washed, but ye are sanctified, but ye are justified in the name of the Lord Jesus, and by the Spirit of our God. (1 Corinthians 6:1–8)

Faith without Works Is Dead

Our bodies are members of Christ.

I woke up on March 28 praising God! Every morning, the Holy Spirit wakes me up very early so that I can have my devotion sometime between three o'clock to four in the morning. After devotion this morning, I was still worshiping God continuously. It was about seven in the morning. I was in deep praise and worship when I started to cry and speak in tongues. My spirit was just ministering to me; that song kept playing in my spirits, "Lead me where my trust is without border / where I walk upon the water / whenever you call me," over and over again. I sat down and continued worshipping when suddenly my nose started bleeding profusely, and then I started coughing up clots of blood! At this present time, I became discombobulated! I don't know what God was doing before then and even now, but I know that he was not on the cross as some people are saying! God left what he was doing to show up for me immediately. Now I can tell you how tangible God is when I turn my eyes toward heaven and said to him: *Oh, God, you tell me that life is in the blood, and why am I losing blood.* Now I cannot comprehend the thoughts of God; when the spoken word exited my mouth, God answered immediately. I said, *Now, God, I will take Jesus's blood, as you said that his blood gives life and life everlasting.* And immediately the blood dried up, and I went and took the communion.

> I am the living bread which came down from heaven: if any man eat of this bread, he shall live for ever: and the bread that I will give is my flesh, which I will give for the life of the world. (John 6:51)

> And he took bread, and gave thanks, and broke it, and gave unto them, saying, This is my body which is given for you: this do in remembrance of me. Likewise He also took the cup after supper, saying, "This cup is the new covenant in My blood, which is shed for you.
> This is my faith in God, and in my everyday life walk a personal relationship that I have with my father in heaven. As I know that Jesus is my Lord and Savior as I walk daily with him. God honor faith! (Luke 22:19–20)

> The centurion answered and said, Lord, I am not worthy that thou shouldest come under my roof: but speak the word only, and my servant shall be healed. For I am a man under authority, having soldiers under me: and I say to this

man, Go, and he goeth; and to another, Come, and he cometh; and to my servant, Do this, and he doeth it. When Jesus heard it, he marvelled, and said to them that followed, Verily I say unto you, I have not found so great faith, no, not in Israel. And I say unto you, That many shall come from the east and west, and shall sit down with Abraham, and Isaac, and Jacob, in the kingdom of heaven. (Matthew 8:7–11)

Even so faith, if it hath not works, is dead, being alone. Yea, a man may say, Thou hast faith, and I have works: shew me thy faith without thy works, and I will shew thee my faith by my works. Thou believest that there is one God; thou doest well: the devils also believe, and tremble. But wilt thou know, O vain man, that faith without works is dead? Was not Abraham our father justified by works, when he had offered Isaac his son upon the altar? (James: 2:17)

Chapter 2

Ridiculous Faith

The Lord Hears Hezekiah's Prayer

In those days Hezekiah was stricken with a terminal illness. The prophet Isaiah son of Amoz visited him and told him, "This is what the Lord says, 'Give instructions to your household, for you are about to die; you will not get well.'" Hezekiah turned his face to the wall and prayed to the Lord, "Please, Lord. Remember how I have served you[b] faithfully and with wholehearted devotion, and how I have carried out your will." Then Hezekiah wept bitterly. (2 Kings 20:1–3)

Go back and tell Hezekiah, the leader of my people, 'This is what the LORD, the God of your father David, says: I have heard your prayer and seen your tears; I will heal you. On the third day from now you will go up to the temple of the LORD. I will add fifteen years to your life. (2 Kings 20:5)

But he that knew not, and did commit things worthy of stripes, shall be beaten with few stripes. For unto whomsoever much is given, of

him shall be much required: and to whom men
have committed much, of him they will ask the
more. (Luke 12:48)

When a robber ambushes a person that has nothing in their
hands, that person has a chance of getting away because there are not
much valuables for a thief to come away with, as a robber is looking
for something of value; and if they realize that this person is empty,
they will not attack them because there's nothing that is of value they
see that they need to waste their time on. If there is nothing in that
person that is worth fighting for, the devil will not torment them.
You know that you are heading in the right direction as we live it
daily when the spiritual battle becomes fierce.

Even so faith, if it hath not works, is dead,
being alone. Yea, a man may say, Thou hast faith,
and I have works: shew me thy faith without thy
works, and I will shew thee my faith by my works.
Thou believest that there is one God; thou doest
well: the devils also believe, and tremble. But wilt
thou know, O vain man, that faith without works
is dead? Was not Abraham our father justified by
works, when he had offered Isaac his son upon
the altar? (James 2: 17–20)

If there isn't a fight spiritually, there is no victory. The person that does not get a fight spiritually is not totally lost; they are
only not connected with God. Everyone who is connected with God
will get a fight from the devil—whether they like it or not. I have
encountered some of the most fierce battles spiritually than other
people because of my anointing that God has given in my life. One
thing I know is that the devil does not fight with his own; he only
tried to delay the plan of God around God's people. If there is no
root under a tree, surely it is only a matter of time before that tree

would wither and die because the root is important to nurture and strengthen that tree.

> I am the vine, you are the branches. He who abides in Me, and I in him, bears much fruit; for without Me you can do nothing. If anyone does not abide in Me, he is cast out as a branch and is withered; and they gather them and throw them into the fire, and they are burned. I you abide in Me, and my words in you, you will ask what you desire, and it shall be done for you. By this My Father is glorified, that you bear much fruit; so you will be My disciples. As the Father loved Me, I also have loved you; abide in My love. If you keep My commandments, you will abide in My love, just as I have kept My Father's commandments and abide in His love. These things I have spoken to you, that My joy may remain in you, and your joy may be fill. (John 15:5–11)

This shadows out unto us that God expects greater returns of duty from some persons than others, and neglect thereof provokes God against them. In the ceremonial law, God required more sacrifices from the rich than from the poor:

> The LORD said to him, "Take YOUR FATHER's bull and a second bull seven years old, and pull down the altar of Baal which belongs to your father and build an altar to the LORD your God on the top of this stronghold in an orderly manner, and take a second bull and offer it. The men of the city were mad. Manifesting a spirit when they saw the altar turned down. BUT this wasn't them—it was the dispossessed Baal spirit working thru them. The devil will attack you thru people when he is under attack thru your obedience.

So…" Then the men of the city said to Joash, "Bring out your son, that he may die, for he has torn down the altar of Baal." (Judges 6:24–30)

Which yet were accepted from the poorer sort of persons. So also under the Gospel, "to whom much is given, of them doth He require the more."

The Ten Virgins!

The Parable of the Ten Virgins

At that time the kingdom of heaven will be like ten virgins who took their lamps and went out to meet the bridegroom. Five of them were foolish and five were wise. The foolish ones took their lamps but did not take any oil with them. The wise ones, however, took oil in jars along with their lamps. The bridegroom was a long time in coming, and they all became drowsy and fell asleep.

At midnight the cry rang out: "Here's the bridegroom! Come out to meet him!" Then all the virgins woke up and trimmed their lamps. The foolish ones said to the wise, "Give us some of your oil; our lamps are going out." "No," they replied, "there may not be enough for both us and you. Instead, go to those who sell oil and buy some for yourselves." (Matthew 25:1–13)

For whoever has will be given more, and they will have an abundance. Whoever does not have, even what they have will be taken from them. And throw that worthless servant outside, into the darkness, where there will be weeping and gnashing of teeth.' (Matthew 25:29–30)

Chapter 3

To Belong

"First I must let you know that God is the only one that is constant in my life. God is the only one that put one up and take one down. God opens a door, and no man can close it. And He closes one door that no man can open it; time and place is in your hands."

There are many things in life that can make you feel like you belong somewhere else. The distinction of being born in a certain place does not make that place your home. It's just the place you were born and raised in. Some are lucky enough to call this place home. Others have to go out and find it. It's more work, but it can be a fun and exciting journey as well. The solution, I find, is to simply do some research into a place that you think may suit you better and just keep going until you've narrowed down the possibilities. Then it's just a matter of visiting that place, deciding if it truly works for you or not, and finding out how to move there. Then work for it as I have done! You don't have to be stuck in one place. You don't have to make excuses for why you should stay there because God has given us free will to go and live any place you feel free in your life.

I am God, your God! I will not rebuke you for your sacrifices or your burnt offerings, which are continually before Me. I will not take a bull from your house, nor goats out of your folds. For every beast of the forest is Mine, and the cattle on a thousand hills. I know all the birds of the mountains, and the wild beasts of the field are

21

> Mine. If I were hungry, I would not tell you; for the world is Mine, and all its fullness. Will I eat the flesh of bulls, or drink the blood of goats? Offer to God thanksgiving, and pay your vows to the Most High, call upon Me in the day of trouble; I will deliver you, and you shall glorify Me. (Psalm 50:7–15)

Since my childhood, I never felt I belonged to my native country, and the feeling has become more and more strong. It is a common feeling as I travel to other countries that draw me to it. The feeling has become stronger when I left Jamaica to seek a better way of life—to have more comfort for my family. It is a common feeling of being tied down without actually being tied. It is normal to feel like you were born in the wrong country because you just don't fit in with the way of life even though you love your culture and other things that give a sense of belonging. Now that I have moved to America, I felt a strong connection to a country that wasn't my own; or that as soon as I visited, it spoke to me in so many different ways.

> Behold, what manner of love the Father hath bestowed upon us, that we should be called the sons of God: therefore the world knoweth us not, because it knew him not. Beloved, now are we the sons of God, and it doth not yet appear what we shall be: but we know that, when he shall appear, we shall be like him; for we shall see him as he is. And every man that hath this hope in him purifieth himself, even as he is pure. Whosoever committeth sin transgresseth also the law: for sin is the transgression of the law. (1 John 3:1–4)

I know that home is where the heart is! What should I do? Since childhood, I never felt I belonged to my native country, and the feeling has become more and more strong. It is a common feeling as I travel to other places around the world. Since childhood, I never felt I belonged to my family as a young girl. When I was born, I was made to understand that my mother was so young. At the age of seventeen, she was so terrified when she gave birth and could not take care of me as a child herself. Her father was a powerful man in that era.

When she had given birth, she had to leave home; and in this process, I was one of the left-behind thoughts also. I was left with my grandmother that had just given birth to her own baby a few months before her own daughter. Even as a baby, my grandmother said she had to nurse me because when she was nursing her baby daughter, I would be crying; so she nursed both of us until I grew up. That was my mother's family!

You should imagine my father's side of the family! They were endowed with power, money, and all the fine things that life has to offer. As a child, I was growing up in two different environments with two different house rules growing up—one on holiday and the other on school days! I was so afraid and yet not afraid when I was going there to my father's family as a child because there was a high style of living on one side and a normal one on the other side. "Don't touch this and don't touch that because you will destroy it." As a child, how could I know what value those things have to them? It brings me to the way food is set up in a grocery store! You break it, you buy it!

There was always a barging for something. Whether clothes, for food, or affection which was overrated, I feel like I don't belong in either of their homes or a country because of my beliefs and/or who I am. I have been to various countries to see if I am going to fit in, but it was not easy to do. I know that I should. But I don't feel like my country is my home, and I need to go somewhere else. I am neither happy nor unhappy, but I love my families even when some of them are not the easiest to get along with and friends who are even unfriendly. And I don't want to leave them before the right time. I have learned that premature birth is a form of abortion. I am waiting for the Lord's time, as I cannot run ahead of God.

Now therefore ye are no more strangers and
foreigners, but fellow citizens with the saints, and

of the household of God; And are built upon the
foundation of the apostles and prophets, Jesus
Christ himself being the chief corner [stone];
In whom all the building fitly framed together
groweth unto an holy temple in the Lord: In
whom ye also are builded together for an habitation of God through the Spirit. (Ephesians
2:19–22)

Could someone have different places around the world that
they think is so comfortable as a place that can be called home? I have
experienced these feelings when I arrived in South Africa in 2018 for
the first time for church. I just cannot get enough of that place that I
just feel because of the worshiping at AMI–Sandton, Johannesburg.
God is saying something to me as always!

Then the word of the LORD came unto
me, saying, Before I formed thee in the belly I
knew thee; and before thou earnest forth out of
the womb I sanctified thee, and I ordained thee
a prophet unto the nations. Then said I, ah, Lord
GOD! behold, I cannot speak: for I am a child.
But the LORD said unto me, say not, I am a child:
for thou shalt go to all that I shall send thee, and
whatsoever I command thee thou shalt speak. Be
not afraid of their faces: for I am with thee to
deliver thee, saith the LORD. Then the LORD put
forth his hand, and touched my mouth. And the
LORD said unto me, Behold, I have put my words
in thy mouth. See, I have this day set thee over
the nations and over the kingdoms, to root out,
and to pull down, and to destroy, and to throw
down, to build, and to plant.
Moreover the word of the LORD came unto
me, saying, Jeremiah, what seest thou? And I said,
I see a rod of an almond tree. Then said the LORD

unto me, thou hast well seen: for I will hasten my word to perform it. And the word of the LORD came unto me the second time, saying, What seest thou? And I said, I see a seething pot; and the face thereof is toward the north. Then the LORD said unto me, out of the north an evil shall break forth upon all the inhabitants of the land.

For, lo, I will call all the families of the kingdoms of the north, saith the LORD; and they shall come, and they shall set every one his throne at the entering of the gates of Jerusalem, and against all the walls thereof round about, and against all the cities of Judah. And I will utter my judgments against them touching all their wickedness, who have forsaken me, and have burned incense unto other gods, and worshipped the works of their own hands. Thou therefore gird up thy loins, and arise, and speak unto them all that I command thee: be not dismayed at their faces, lest I confound thee before them. 18 For, behold, I have made thee this day a defenced city, and an iron pillar, and brasen walls against the whole land, against the kings of Judah, against the princes thereof, against the priests thereof, and against the people of the land. (Jeremiah 1:5–18)

Even the prophet Jeremiah said, Amen: the LORD do so: the LORD perform thy words which thou hast prophesied, to bring again the vessels of the LORD's house, and all that is carried away captive, from Babylon into this place. Nevertheless hear thou now this word that I speak in thine ears, and in the ears of all the people; The prophets that have been before me and before thee of old prophesied both against many countries, and against great kingdoms, of war, and of evil, and of pestilence.

The prophet which prophesieth of peace, when the word of the prophet shall come to pass, then shall the prophet be known, that the LORD hath truly sent him. Then Hananiah the prophet took the yoke from off the prophet Jeremiah's neck, and brake it. And Hananiah spake in the presence of all the people, saying, Thus saith the LORD; Even so will I break the yoke of Nebuchadnezzar king of Babylon from the neck of all nations within the space of two full years. And the prophet Jeremiah went his way. (Jeremiah 28:6)

Every place that the sole of your foot shall tread upon, that have I given unto you, as I said unto Moses. From the wilderness and this Lebanon even unto the great river, the river Euphrates, all the land of the Hittites, and unto the great sea toward the going down of the sun, shall be your coast. There shall not any man be able to stand before thee all the days of thy life: as I was with Moses, [so] I will be with thee: I will not fail thee, nor forsake thee. 6 Be strong and of a good courage: for unto this people shalt thou divide for an inheritance the land, which I sware unto their fathers to give them. (Joshua 1)

Only be thou strong and very courageous, that thou mayest observe to do according to all the law, which Moses my servant commanded thee: turn not from it [to] the right hand or [to] the left, that thou mayest prosper whithersoever thou goest. This book of the law shall not depart out of thy mouth; but thou shalt meditate therein day and night, that thou mayest observe to do according to all that is written therein: for then thou shalt make thy way prosperous, and then thou shalt have good success. Have not I commanded thee? Be strong and of a good courage; be not afraid, neither be thou dismayed: for the LORD thy God [is] with thee whithersoever thou goest. (Joshua 4)

I love America! As I step off the plane and walk into the terminal at the airport at JFK International, I know that God is looking out for me! I always sing the anthem, even at my job. The way the snowflakes fall with a slow pace, the whiteness of it all, and the wind and the cold and the calmness of the snow upon the head as it settled on the breath of the people as they walk in the snow—all you could hear is the wind whispering in your ears there. It's so different from my home but somehow familiar and somehow beautiful in some way, and it strikes my soul somewhere in a manner I don't understand. I put my hands up in the air and feel the freeness of the air as my heart beats a million beats per second; my mind is flying like an eagle with wings outstretched above the ocean, thanking God!

> God bless America, land that I love
> Stand beside her and guide her
> Through the night with the light from above
> From the mountains to the prairies
> To the oceans white with foam
> God bless America, my home sweet home
> God bless America, land that I love
> Stand beside her and guide her
> Through the night with the light from above
> From the mountains to the prairies
> To the oceans white with foam
> God bless America, my home sweet home
> From the mountains to the prairies
> To the oceans white with foam
> God bless America, my home sweet home
> God bless America, my home sweet home
> (Kate Smith, "God Bless America")

Chapter 4

It's time for the church to arise again! Judgment must begin in the house of the Lord. Do not keep silent as God calls us into a place of humility and love for one another.

Do you know how many persons are dead and buried with secrets that are an asset to another person? I do! Let not the way a person think defy you! A lot of people would tell you today that they love you and all that you are going through. Put on a silver platter before them; give them the chance to examine it and let you know what they think of your situation. When they are examining it, they wait until you are dead to give the answer! I don't want to be one of those persons. The Bible tells me that there is no repentance in the grave. So whatsoever I am about to give to a person or invest in another, I will do the will of God now!

I'm at the point with God where I am looking for peace and tranquility! As I search for the deep things of God, pre adventure of the things to be mature as there could be abortion on the existence of the date before maturity; it's not good before its mature date. That it can come to full maturity.

Yesterday was a testimony. I called one of my daughters in South Africa to see if she was doing well, had gone to service, and had food. She stated that she had no data to watch the service and only a little food left from her reserve from the package the church delivered. I was sick in my stomach to know that there is so much food in my home and my own children have enough to eat as they are all grown up now. I was sitting down doing my pedicure, and my beloved daughter did not have much food to eat—that was my thought! I was done, and there was forty-five dollars left in my bag. I looked on my left, and the check cashing was there. I went in and took everything out and asked the cashier how much it was to send the money to my daughter. She told me, and I told her to send the funds to the name I gave her of my daughter. After I sent that money to my daughter, I walked over to the counter to take a picture to send her the code, and there were about ten scratch-off tickets that were waiting to be thrown in the garbage. And I just looked over. And there I saw on one of the tickets two-time, and the rest was not scratched off. I picked up all the tickets and took them home with me.

I sat down at the dining table and took out the tickets I brought home and started to scratch them off, and there under the two-time was a twenty. So there I got forty dollars; and on another I scratched, there was ten, another three, and another five dollars. God surprised me speedily!

Satan Is After Your Seed!

Before I had any idea how seeds work, I was always a protector over my children, the fruit of my womb. They are God's reward. I have sown seed into the work of God from I was a small child. I have sown into so many ministries around the world without stopping it cannot be counted. "Now I know the use of my seeds."

Very, truly, I tell you, except a grain of kernel or wheat falls into the ground and dies, it remains only a single seed; but if it die, it produces many seeds. (John 12:24)

Wilt thou trust him, because his strength is great? or wilt thou leave thy labour to him? Wilt thou believe him, that he will bring home thy seed, and gather it into thy barn?

We are in a time now that the Lord is opening the eyes of his people to walk in our inheritance that He has promise to the chosen generation! Seed could be our children or; our tithes and offering unto the Lord our God; It could be a seed to birth a miracle, as everyone must know that God honor faith. The Vows, that we make is also very important, and all things that please God that is good, and are aligned with the purposes of God. (Job 39:11)

Sojourn in this land, and I will be with thee, and will bless thee; for unto thee, and unto thy seed, I will give all these countries, and I will perform the oath which I sware unto Abraham thy father; and I will make thy seed to multiply as the stars of heaven, and will give unto thy seed all these countries; and in thy seed shall all the nations of the earth be blessed; because that Abraham obeyed my voice, and kept my charge, my commandments, my statutes, and my laws. And Isaac dwelt in Gerar: and the men of the place asked him of his wife; and he said, she is my sister: for he feared to say, she is my wife; lest, said he, the men of the place should kill me for Rebekah; because she was fair to look upon. (Genesis 26:4)

Now he that ministereth seed to the sower both minister bread for your food, and multiply your seed sown, and increase the fruits of your righteousness; Being enriched in every thing to all bountifulness, which causeth through us thanksgiving to God. For the administration of this service not only supplieth the wants of the want of the saints, but is abundant also by many thanksgivings unto God; Whiles by the experiment of this ministration they glorify God for your professed subjection unto the gospel of Christ, and for your liberal distribution unto them, and unto all men; And by their prayer for you, which long after you for the exceeding grace of God in you.

Thanks be unto God for his unspeakable gift. (2 Corinthians 10:15)

Moreover the word of the LORD came to Jeremiah, saying, Considerest thou not what this people have spoken, saying, The two families which the LORD hath chosen, he hath even cast them off? thus they have despised my people, that they should be no more a nation before them. Thus saith the LORD; If my covenant be not with day and night, and if I have not appointed the ordinances of heaven and earth; Then will I cast away the seed of Jacob, and David my servant, so that I will not take any of his seed to be rulers over the seed of Abraham, Isaac, and Jacob: for I will cause their captivity to return, and have mercy on them. (Jeremiah 33:23–26)

Now I beseech you, brethren, mark them which cause divisions and offences contrary to the doctrine and there appeared a great wonder in heaven; a woman clothed with the sun, and the moon under her feet, and upon her head a crown of twelve stars: And she being with child cried, travailing in birth, and pained to be delivered. And there appeared another wonder in heaven; and behold a great red dragon, having seven heads and ten horns, and seven crowns upon his heads. And his tail drew the third part of the stars of heaven, and did cast them to the earth: and the dragon stood before the woman which was ready to be delivered, for to devour her child as soon as it was born.

And she brought forth a man child, who was to rule all nations with a rod of iron: and her child was caught up unto God, and to his throne. And the woman fled into the wilderness, where she hath a place prepared of God, that they should feed her there a thousand two hundred and threescore days. And there was war in heaven: Michael and his angels fought against the dragon; and the dragon fought and his angels, and prevailed not; neither was their place found any more in heaven. And the great dragon was cast out, that old serpent, called the Devil, and Satan, which deceiveth the whole world: he was cast out into the earth, and his angels were cast out with him. (Revelations 1:9)

I have never stopped sowing seeds in the house of God. There was a time when I don't even have much to go on, but something for years speaks in my heart to continue sowing my seeds. "Every impossibility is a seed to give birth to a miracle."

Then Jesus sent the multitude away, and went into the house: and his disciples came unto him, saying, Declare unto us the parable of the tares of the field. He answered and said unto them, He that soweth the good seed is the Son of man; The field is the world; the good seed are the children of the kingdom; but the tares are the children of the wicked one; The enemy that sowed them is the devil; the harvest is the end of the world; and the reapers are the angels. As therefore the tares are gathered and burned in the fire; so shall it be in the end of this world. The Son of man shall send forth his angels, and they shall gather out of his kingdom all things that offend, and them which do iniquity. (Mathew 13:36–41)

While the earth remaineth, seedtime and harvest, and cold and heat, and summer and winter, and day and night shall not cease. The said, So is the kingdom of God, as if a man should cast seed into the ground. (Genesis 8:22)

And should sleep, and rise night and day, and the seed should spring and grow up, he knoweth not how. For the earth bringeth forth fruit of herself; first the blade, then the ear, after that the full corn in the ear. But when the fruit is brought forth, immediately he putteth in the sickle, because the harvest is come. (Mark 4:26–29)

Give, and it shall be given unto you; good measure, pressed down, and shaken together, and running over, shall men give into your bosom. For with the same measure that ye mete withal it shall be measured to you again. (Luke 6:38)

Be not deceived; God is not mocked: for whatsoever a man soweth, that shall he also reap.

Thus saith the LORD of hosts; Let your hands be strong, ye that hear in these days these words by the mouth of the prophets, which were in the day that the foundation of the house of the LORD of hosts was laid, that the temple might be built. For before these days there was no hire for man, nor any hire for beast; neither was there any peace to him that went out or came in because of the affliction: for I set all men every one against his neighbour. But now I will not be unto the residue of this people as in the former days, saith the LORD of hosts.

For the seed shall be prosperous; the vine shall give her fruit, and the ground shall give her increase, and the heavens shall give their dew; and

I will cause the remnant of this people to possess all these things. And it shall come to pass, that as ye were a curse among the heathen, O house of Judah, and house of Israel; so will I save you, and ye shall be a blessing: fear not, but let your hands be strong. For thus saith the LORD of hosts; As I thought to punish you, when your fathers provoked me to wrath, saith the LORD of hosts, and I repented not: So again have I thought in these days to do well unto Jerusalem and to the house of Judah: fear ye not. (Galatians 6:7)

And Jesus knew their thoughts, and said unto them, Every kingdom divided against itself is brought to desolation; and every city or house divided against itself shall not stand: And if Satan cast out Satan, he is divided against himself; how shall then his kingdom stand? And if I by Beelzebub cast out devils, by whom do your children cast them out? therefore they shall be your judges. But if I cast out devils by the Spirit of God, then the kingdom of God is come unto you. Or else how can one enter into a strong man's house, and spoil his goods, except he first bind the strong man? And then he will spoil his house. (Matthew 12:26–29)

Chapter 5

Altars and Their Powers

"I will leave the how, the when, and the why to God."
Before you build any type of altars, you must know that there was not one in the place that you are going to build it. Because altars cannot just be destroyed by moving things around, it must be broken down by prayers and be destroyed. I have encountered some of the most diabolical altars that destroyed a lot of growth in my life and delayed the process of God's blessing in my life.

When I left Jamaica, I had no understanding of how altars work as a Christian. I was very naive, but GOD helped me know the things that let me escape the prongs of the devil that was making my home and life a living nightmare. The sleepless nights and the unhappy feelings I was used to made it seem natural in those days. All I could think about is my children and their well-being. Demons were never talked about much as we think that it was a tale of the older generation who only tells us things in parables.

My home was a disaster daily with strange things happening day and night. I did not realize how I had so many spiritual battles until I had my last daughter. I could not sleep, and my baby kept crying all night.

I called for my church sisters to come and pray in my home, and they ran to my house. Do you think I could ever forget this day? That was a day to remember. I am so serious that this is something that happened to me in Jamaica in the nineties. Not forgetting that I am a Christian and living right, I would say. Somehow I was one of the devil's target! So afraid and don't want to stay at home alone,

I started to think that if I ran away from Jamaica, I would leave the demons behind. I was so wrong and was not even aware of it that only casting out the devil can help me or anyone who seeks deliverance. There was a time that we called the Catholic priest to come to my home to pray, and when he came in with frankincense and myrrh and holy water, the evil left until the place was with the evil's presence again. All my years, I am a praying woman, and I think this is the only reason why the devil could not have its way in my file and my children's life.

I left Jamaica, and I am living in America now.

Years went by, and I am living in America with my husband and children and their families. I built an altar. No one told me about an altar. I had placed things that are important to me on my altar in my home to God with prayers. In 2012, I had so many spiritual battles that were not a joke to get rid of. At the church I was attending, Church of God of Prophecy, we had a Daniel fasting for twenty-one days. I joined, and this was my first time doing such a long fasting. But I tried my best to stay in as well as I could. At this time, those people who were doing spiritual things to me had no idea that I was aware of their wickedness. One of them called me and gave me an envelope with money in it, and as soon as the money touched my hand, the Holy Spirit spoke to me. And just as I reached home, I said Lord they had offered this money to their God.

I am offering it to you as I know that you are the king of kings and the Lord of Lords. I left the envelope on my altar home until the Sunday when I took it and left it at the church where that altar is also built on JESUS CHRIST. When they opened the envelope, they called me to thank me for such generous offering. I was only doing what the Holy Spirit instructed me to do in being obedient because I have learned it is better than the sacrifice that I made.

"If it does not cost you, it will not pay you." On my twentieth day of fasting, they called me because all hell broke loose in their home. Because GOD is a miracle-working GOD, I got a call from one of them, and I asked the Lord to please answer and speak for me. And God did.

The phone rang, I answered, "Hello, how may I help you!"

He said, "Can you come to take care of my sister for me. I don't know what happened to her. They have put her on oxygen when she went to the doctor, and I don't want anyone else to care for her now."

I know that the sister is not that old because I took care of their mother, and the mother was only in her eighties. They fought me day and night for nothing—correction—they thought that their mother would leave everything to me and my sister.

However, I know that she had left me something in her *will,* and both of her children have not read it openly for anyone to know the truth about everything. But God has delivered me out of the hands of the enemy.

I replied promptly and said, "I am not available, but if you would like someone else, I can send them to you as soon as possible."

He was shocked and said, "I don't want anyone else, only you."

I hung up, and a week later, I heard that the wicked sister passed on. And he alone in the family knows how much money his mother left for me even when he kept the gifts and still behaving as if I don't know, but I leave everything to GOD who sees all things and judges them as that it was already told to me by his mother.

Now I lost interest in doing anything for that family anymore and had not heard from them for four years. Then my phone rang four years later, and the man called me to take care of his friend. I sent a woman, and he accepted her. A day later he called me, and I asked him how is his family. And he said they are well. He said to me that whatever God or thing I am praying to is powerful.

Chapter 6

Altars and How They're Defeated

This is a true story about my family and me—how I used my altar in our home, family business, and my career by defying more demonic spirits and building a family altar.

I am just a simple person going about my business every day. After working for people all my life, I decided to open a home care because this is a good business to do, as other big companies are scraping up the best of everything including every patient as they're released from the hospital and nursing homes.

I maximize my steps with great strides as I walk to church just around the corner every Sunday a couple of blocks from where I live. Service starts at 10:00 a.m. I just can't wait to get there for praise and worship as glorifying God is what I live for. I am a person who spends my time talking with God, praying my love for God, and working hard; but every time his harvest was due, a demonic spirit of strife would come and rip off not only me but also this entire household.

God actually is my refuge, a very present help in the time of my trouble, to address this problem by using frustration to a level that drives me to prayer where I did not know how to sleep because of the evil in my home and the devastation of my workers. When I send them to cover a job, sometimes the person I send them to would keep calling for someone else because they don't want that person, and this is what I would face with daily. And they lodged so many complaints. From every angle, there is a problem that stems from evil.

I am a worrier for God, so this is a norm when you are fighting demons night and day. Patients hold on to my finance from the job

38

that was done, but they refuse to pay for the services that they already received.

For four years, I devoted my life and time to spend with GOD after going through the trauma of spiritual wickedness in almost everything I put my hands on. My entire substance in my home has been diluted in a solution that has no value! I could feel the air with my hands as the darkness took control of the atmosphere around my entire existence including my family. The Lord told the youth that God was with him and this man would change the nation with just a *handful* (a remnant)—rallying them "as one man"!

Whatever cannot defeat your altar cannot defeat you, as I was taught in a church conference after going to South Africa by a man of God!

Chapter 7

Breaking Altars Are Very Necessary

And it came to pass the same night, that the Lord said unto him, Take thy father's young bullock, even the second bullock of seven years old, and throw down the altar of Baal that thy father hath, and cut down the grove that is by it.

The LORD said to him, "Take YOUR FATHER'S bull and a second bull seven years old, and pull down the altar of Baal which belongs to your father and build an altar to the LORD your God on the top of this stronghold in an orderly manner, and take a second bull and offer it. The men of the city were mad. Manifesting a spirit when they saw the altar turned down. BUT this wasn't them—it was the dispossessed Baal spirit working thru them. The devil will attack you thru people when he is under attack thru your obedience. So..." Then the men of the city said to Joash, "Bring out your son, that he may die, for he has torn down the altar of Baal." (Judges 6:24–30)

God did this to let them know that he is God Almighty!

But Joash said to all who stood against him, "Will you contend for Baal, or will you deliver him? Whoever will plead for him shall be put to death by morning. If he is a god, let him contend for himself, because someone has torn down his altar." (Judges 6:31–32)

Take heed to thyself, lest thou make a covenant with the inhabitants of the land whither thou goest, lest it be for a snare in the midst of thee: But ye shall destroy their altars, break their images, and cut down their groves: For thou shalt worship no other god: for the Lord, whose name is Jealous, is a jealous God. (Exodus 34:12)

Ye shall utterly destroy all the places, wherein the nations which ye shall possess served their gods, upon the high mountains, and upon the hills, and under every green tree: 3 And ye shall overthrow their altars, and break their pillars, and burn their groves with fire; and ye shall hew down the graven images of their gods, and destroy the names of them out of that place. (Deuteronomy 3:2)

And all the people of the land went into the house of Baal, and brake it down; his altars and his images brake they in pieces thoroughly, and slew Mattan the priest of Baal before the altars. And the priest appointed officers over the house of the Lord. (2 Kings 11:18)

And the altars that were on the top of the upper chamber of Ahaz, which the kings of Judah had made, and the altars which Manasseh had made in the two courts of the house of the Lord, did the king beat down, and brake them down from thence, and cast the dust of them into the brook Kidron. (2 Kings 23:12)

"After breaking altars, you need to build an altar to the Lord God Almighty."

It was in September of 2018. I was watching my regular church programs, and I got kicked off from Jimmy Swaggart live. I was confused but continued to watch the channel anyway! After that program, I know that was what I was looking for all these years serving God, and I want to be a part of this thing. Whatsoever it is, I am going to find that place. I don't think I have ever been compelled to find anything in my life until now.

Chapter 8

Building an Altar

"An altar must signify something—as everything is spiritual."

Then he proceeded from there to the mountain on the east of Bethel, and pitched his tent, with Bethel on the west and Ai on the east; and there he built an altar to the Lord and called upon the name of the Lord. (Genesis 12:8–9)

To the place of the altar which he had made there formerly; and there Abram called on the name of the Lord. (Genesis 13:4)

Then Abram moved his tent and came and dwelt by the oaks of Mamre, which are in Hebron, and there he built an altar to the Lord. (Genesis 13:18)

Then they came to the place of which God had told him; and Abraham built the altar there and arranged the wood, and bound his son Isaac and laid him on the altar, on top of the wood. (Genesis 22:9)

So he built an altar there and called upon the name of the Lord, and pitched his tent there;

and there Isaac's servants dug a well. (Genesis 26:25)

Then he erected there an altar and called it El-Elohe-Israel. (Genesis 33:20)

Then God said to Jacob, "Arise, go up to Bethel and live there, and make an altar there to God, who appeared to you when you fled from your brother Esau." (Genesis 35:1)

Source: https://bible.knowing-jesus.com/topics/Building-Altars

Chapter 9

The Mind of God Is in Us

"We are God's creation, and as Christ is, so are we. And we must walk in his example so that the world will know that God is who he said he is! I have a mind like Christ."

What man that is he who desired to live life and not wanting to enjoy the bountiful lifestyle he created for himself? Now look at the way God created everything beautiful, and man destroyed most of the things that make his creation happy! There are numerous things that we can attest to that we enjoy from God—the breath of life, our family, beautiful beaches, fishing, rafting, and I could go on and on!

Even though I have an effective altar, I did not know it was effective and how powerful it was until I heard the teaching of how the altar will need to break down before I could build one. The things in your life, whether they are good or bad, that you don't know can certainly hurt you if it is bad. I did not know anything about breaking down these altars, or building one, but I did. When God is teaching you, it makes no sense then—until you get the revelation.

However, it took me years to get that revelation as a baby drinks its milk. As a baby grows, everything around their life changes. As I grow in Christ, so does the knowledge that God gave to me before I have gone to South Africa and met with the man of God. I can say that these trips have given me a firm foundation of how God is almighty and have made my eyes open of the things that have been revealed to his people by his prophet.

We are entering a time when they who know their God shall be strong and do exploits. It is not faith alone but the works that bear fruits and the TRUTH YOU KNOW that sets you free from bondage and the works of the wicked! Therefore know that your God is real, and in the power of his might, he is with us. Do not believe every spirit but TEST the spirits as the Word of God said whether you think that they are of God.

> I said again, I am with you until the end of time for I know the plans I have for you, the thoughts that I think toward you, saith the Lord, thoughts of peace, and not of evil, to give you an expected end. Then shall you call upon me, and you shall go and pray unto me, and I will answer you. And you shall seek me, and find me, when you shall search for me with all of your heart. And I will be found of you, saith the Lord: and I will turn away your captivity, and I will gather you from all the nations, and from all the places whither I have driven you, saith the Lord; and I will bring you again into the place whence I caused you to be carried away captive. (Jeremiah 29)

Set yourself aside as a peculiar people as the Lord has chosen us. Now that we are enlightened in his words, we can go and build an altar to our GOD without reservation.

As you set yourself aside, I am building my church for the last days. It is not an ark or an exit but a dwelling place of living stones called together as a habitation of God in the earth—a tabernacle of David where you can find me in the place of worship. Call unto me, and I will answer you when you seek me with all of your heart.

> For I am giving you access to an open heaven to walk under in your battle—praises in the night—revelation in the contradiction of your circumstance, and even access to my counsel wisdom in the place of contention. You will

build a 'thin place' for intimacy with me in sep-
aration hour. For I am building MY church, my
ecclesia in the earth, and you will come together
'as one man'—not as separate but AS ONE. And
the Lord shall MULTIPLY your strength beyond
your size, and so shall you overcome and occupy
the land which I give to you. Even a land filled
with giants.

I called him "God-man." Pastor Alph Lukau is one of the most
prophetic anointing person I have ever met. His teaching is a burn-
ing fire that needs more wood to consume the gravity of the cold in
the room and adjusted the heat temperature of the anointing upon
each sons and daughters of God, our spiritual father at AMI.

Chapter 10

"Yahweh-shammah." I SEE YOU EVERYWHERE! (Ezekiel 48:35)

I was wondering how I became so spiritually attached to God when I started getting attacked from every area of my life. In 2007, I was working in one of NorthShore hospitals. I met with a patient in a room, and this encounter has changed my life.

At sunrise, each day was very special because I was there, and she looked forward to seeing me every day. The nights had become very hard for her because she missed my presence and at night as she lay in bed, knowing that I would not be there. A daughter, a friend, and a confidant—I was like a tower of strength to her in her existence, she told me. I entered the room each morning, and there she is lighted up, sitting on the bed and waiting patiently for me to come in!

It was something so special from God knowing that my way-maker has opened a new door for me and that no man can close it, and my perception is that my open door is with this Jewish woman. I specified this because I am a Jew circumcised by the heart, as the Word of God said.

> Now, Israel, what does the LORD your God require from you, but to fear the LORD your God, to walk in all His ways and love Him, and to serve the LORD your God with all your heart and with all your soul, and to keep the LORD's commandments and His statutes which I am commanding you today for your good? Behold, to the LORD your God belong heaven and the highest heavens, the earth and all that is in it. Yet

on your fathers did the LORD set His affection to love them, and He chose their descendants after them, even you above all peoples, as it is this day. So circumcise your heart, and stiffen your neck no longer. For the LORD your God is the God of gods and the Lord of lords, the great the mighty, and the awesome God who does not show partiality nor take a bribe. He executes justice for the orphan and the widow, and shows His love for the alien by giving him food and clothing. So show your love for the alien, for you were aliens in the land of Egypt. You shall fear the LORD your God; you shall serve Him and cling to Him, and you shall swear by His name. He is your praise and He is your God, who has done these great and awesome things for you which your eyes have seen. Your fathers went down to Egypt seventy persons in all, and now the LORD your God has made you as numerous as the stars of heaven. (Deuteronomy 10:12–22)

But I will come to you after I go through Macedonia, for I am going through Macedonia, And perhaps I will stay with you, or even spend the winter, so that you may send me on my way wherever I may go. For I do not wish to see you now just in passing; for I hope to remain with you for some time, if the Lord permits. But I will remain in Ephesus until Pentecost; For a wide door for effective service has opened to me, and there are many adversaries. (1 Corinthians 16:5)

I know thy works: behold, I have set before thee an open door, and no man can shut it: for thou hast a little strength, and hast kept my word, and hast not denied my name. (Revelation 3:8)

Notwithstanding to impose the will of God in my life, I took the patient home to her house where I assigned home care persons to help with her active daily living. I can tell you that my strength cometh from the Lord. At this time, I am working at the hospital and at the patient's home. It is like having fourteen days in one week as there was no day off from work. This helps me remember that David's words to God more and more! I would start to have spiritual fights with people from all angles, but I handle it very well with wisdom. I have never told anyone that I was a Christian following the teachings of Jesus Christ daily. Some people in life are in it for what they can get out of your work, and others will try to derail your life path if they can! These are things I have seen for myself. I have led my life as a testimony to others who don't know that I am their worst nightmare. Quote and quote! As I can use this phrase from a man of God who is powerful in God who said, "I am the best friend to have and the worse adversity altogether."

> Wisdom [is] the principal thing; [therefore] get wisdom: and with all thy getting get understanding. Exalt her, and she shall promote thee: she shall bring thee to honour, when thou dost embrace her. She shall give to thine head an ornament of grace: a crown of glory shall she deliver to thee. Hear, O my son, and receive my sayings; and the years of thy life shall be many. I have taught thee in the way of wisdom; I have led thee in right paths. (Proverbs 4:7)

There were days when I have so many problems to deal with going to work I get up and can't focus on things that are in my daily routine. I would just sing and put gospel songs on and just started driving and don't get carried away with the things I cannot figure out. I pulled up in front of her house, and there are groups of black crows spreading out across the lady's front lawn. And as soon as I entered her house, I felt the blow. I am rooted and grounded in Christ in love, and I will not be shaken!

This is a true testimony also: I was driving, and I looked both ways where the traffic was coming from when I came out and continued driving until I came to a stop at a red light. A bus pulled up to my left side, and the driver rolled his window down and said to me, "Whatsoever you are praying to, do not stop because only him or that kept me from hitting your jeep a while ago." I had no clue what he was saying because I looked both ways before I came out on the road. I told him that I did not see him, and I know there and then that the angel of the Lord had carried me safely!

The Weapons of Our Warfare!

Now I Paul myself beseech you by the meekness and gentleness of Christ who in presence am base among you, but being absent am bold toward you: But I beseech you, that I may not be bold when I am present with that confidence, with which I think to be bold against some, which think of us as if we walked according to the flesh. For though we walk in the flesh, we do not war after the flesh: (For the weapons of our warfare are not carnal, but mighty through God to the pulling down of strong holds;) Casting down imaginations, and every high thing that exalts itself against the knowledge of God, and bringing into captivity every thought to the obedience of Christ; And having in a readiness to revenge all disobedience, when your obedience is fulfilled. Be strong in the Lord. (2 Corinthians 10)

Finally, my brothers, be strong in the Lord, and in the power of his might. Put on the whole armor of God, that you may be able to stand against the wiles of the devil.

For we wrestle not against flesh and blood, but against principalities, against powers, against the rulers of the darkness of this world, against spiritual wickedness in high places. Why take to you the whole armor of God, that you may be able to withstand in the evil day, and having done all, to stand. Stand therefore, having your loins girt about with truth, and having on the breast-plate of righteousness; And your feet shod with the preparation of the gospel of peace; Above all, taking the shield of faith, with which you shall be able to quench all the fiery darts of the wicked. And take the helmet of salvation, and the sword of the Spirit, which is the word of God. (Ephesians 6:10)

God is our refuge and strength, a very present help in trouble.

Therefore will not we fear, though the earth be removed, and though the mountains be carried into the middle of the sea; Though the waters thereof roar and be troubled, though the mountains shake with the swelling thereof. Selah. (Psalm 46:1)

For who [is] God save the LORD? or who [is] a rock save our God? [It is] God that girdeth me with strength, and maketh my way perfect. He maketh my feet like hinds' [feet], and setteth me upon my high places. (Psalm 18:31)

Final Chapter of All

"This is the first in my life I feel like I belong as a person and a Christian. Everything that I was looking for all over the place, and I was running around the world to and fro to find a common ground where I could worship the Lord and how I was feeling without reservation."

The Cry of People

God, rescue your people we are hearing from all over the world from these impossible things that they couldn't make sense of. When God made Adam, God said it was very good, and God sees that it was not good for man to be alone. So he put Adam to sleep and took a rib from Adam and made Eve his helpmate.

I thank God that he is not like man that he may lie or the son of man that he will confess. Not knowing that the way that men do things are far from how God works. Sometimes the things God does do not make sense! When did men become so wicked and vile to one another that they would destroy the things of God's world for only an exaltation of themselves. What can a man give in exchange for his soul? Or can a man gain the world and lose his soul? The question remains unanswered. This plan was not in the plan of God because God so love the world that he gave his only begotten Son. We should have lived and live more abundantly!

Instead of the plans of God to activate in man's life, they strayed, and Satan saw the opening where he could invest his wicked intention into people who are not aligned with the plans and purpose of God. When God looks down and sees that the righteousness of man is not what it should be, God turns to his mercy seat and sees his only Son, Jesus, and remembers his covenant with Abraham that he should not worship any other god. The pulchritude of what God prepared for those who love him outweighs the ones who are unrighteous when God remembers his covenant with Noah every time he puts the rainbow in the sky!

> "For I know the plans I have for you," declares the Lord, "plans to prosper and not to harm you, plans to give you hope and a future." (Jeremiah 29:11)

> This know also, that in the last days perilous times shall come. For men shall be lovers of their own selves, covetous, boasters, proud, blasphemers, disobedient to parents, unthankful, unholy, Without natural affection, trucebreakers, false accusers, incontinent, fierce, despisers of those that are good, Traitors, heady, highminded, lovers of pleasures more than lovers of God; Having a form of godliness, but denying the power thereof: from such turn away. For of this sort are they which creep into houses, and lead captive silly women laden with sins, led away with divers lusts, ever learning, and never able to come to the knowledge of the truth. (2 Timothy 3:1)

I know where I belong as I am walking in the beauty of holiness in Jesus Christ, who is the author and finisher of my faith. As in faith, I know that the steps of a good man are ordered by the Lord. "The Lord keepeth my foot from falling, not one of my bones will be broken."

Breaking altars and building altars and doing it from the city of the skull, which is the altar of God, our altars can be effective just as it was two thousand years ago! God is holding us in the palm of his hands and looks at us continually. Nothing can escape God as he said, "If you make your bed in hell, behold I am there. If you flee to the uttermost part of the sea, even there I will be."

Some of us start out on the wrong foot but find our footing in the right place when we find God and have a relationship with him. Even virgins are pure, and I cannot understand why some were wise and some were foolish because they were all virgins—innocent and pure! God makes all things new and works it out for them who love him.

> Nevertheless the foundation of God standeth sure, having this seal, The Lord knoweth them that are his. And, let every one that nameth the name of Christ depart from iniquity. (2 Timothy 2:19)

The seeds of a woman will bruise the head of the serpent—that's what the Bible tells me. My seeds that are laid at the altars of God speak over my children, marriage, family, friends, business, and everything; God said I would have! My seeds in the ground speak louder than any enemy's voice that I have heard. "Witchcraft can only overpower a person when they are spiritually blind." I have encountered the power of God. How mighty are the works of God's hands. I know that whatsoever I do not fight and defeat, my children will have to fight, and whatsoever can't defeat your altar cannot defeat me!

Then the words of the Lord came to Jeremiah, saying, "Behold, I'm the Lord, the God of all flesh. Is there anything too hard for me to do?"

THE END!

About the Author

She is known as a prayer warrior who receives answers from God. She is a minister of Christ for five years but was a Christian for an uncountable number of years after spending at least seven hours per day with God. As a family-oriented person, Joan Parris spends more time with her family and loved ones. She is also called God squad by her spouse. She spends time praying with people who call her and tell her explicitly that the Lord instructed them to call her for prayer. Joan Parris does a lot of midnight prayers, as this is what she does best. (However, she does pray morning and noon also.) Joan Parris tried her best to pray in the area according to what the Lord said.

Joan Parris goes around and adopts other people's children wherever she goes, not by changing their names or habitations but only give to their lives and give them a better way that they can live more comfortably. Joan Parris has found some children who are very prayerful and thankful to God, and she loves that because she lives a godly life.

Joan Parris lives her life on the foundation of the Word of God! Lots of miracles are happening daily now in people's lives, and those who prayed with her get their prayers answered as God is a prayer-answering God! They are awakened by new miracles every day from God as he surprises his people daily!